A Bible Catechism

Hear, my son, your father's instruction, and forsake not your mother's teaching.
(Proverbs 1:8)

Dr. Charles R. Vogan Jr.

ISBN   978-0-6151-3932-6

Ravenbrook Publishers

A subsidiary of

Shenandoah Bible Ministries

———————— ✄ ————————

www.shenbible.org

Contents

Introduction

The Church, according to Paul, is <u>one</u> people who believe in <u>one</u> truth. They are one in Christ, which means that they share the same life in the Spirit. Supposedly they should agree with each other at least on the basics of the faith.

But since the birth of the Protestant movement there have been innumerable splits among the people of God over doctrine. Christians can't seem to agree about what the Bible teaches – though supposedly the truth there is plain to see, and they all have the same Spirit revealing that truth to them.

Many times the cause for disagreement is simply over wording. Wars have been fought over how religious truths should be worded, as if the Lord favors only those who have their doctrine wrapped up in literary perfection! But many times disagreement in churches have arisen because not everyone is familiar with the basics of the faith. Not everyone has been taught yet about what the foundation truths of the Gospel are. Yet even complex theological arguments are based first on the basic truths of the Bible. If everyone agreed on those simple truths, there would probably be more peace and agreement on the more difficult questions since everyone would be standing on the same foundation.

A Foundation

These basic beliefs serve several purposes: **first**, they are the minimum truths that a Christian should know in order to be able to say that he understands the Gospel of Christ. Like a foundation of a house, we have to have a certain amount of foundation of truth under us so that we won't sink under temptation, oppression, or deception.

> Therefore everyone who hears these words of mine and puts them into practice is like a wise man who built his house on the rock. The rain came down, the streams rose, and the winds blew and beat against that house; yet it did not fall, because it had its foundation on the rock. But everyone who hears these words of mine and does not put them into practice is like a foolish man who built his house on sand. The rain came down, the streams rose, and the winds blew and beat against that house, and it fell with a great crash. (Matthew 7:24-27)

Knowing these truths will be like pulling out the right tool, or turning to a particularly effective weapon, when the time of need arrives. It will be a nasty surprise to discover, for example, when we come under fire from the enemy of our souls, that we don't have the information that we need to make an informed decision or to take appropriate action. Our lives are at stake here; it's wise to prepare ahead of time for the times of great need.

> Go to the ant, you sluggard; consider its ways and be wise! It has no commander, no overseer or ruler, yet it stores its provisions in summer and gathers its food at harvest. (Proverbs 6:6-8)

And in learning these truths, we are learning about the kind of world that we live in. Children spend a lot of time learning about this physical world so that they can grow up as responsible adults and make their own way in it. Spiritually speaking, Christians are learning the same kinds of things about the spiritual world that they are in. The foundation facts of the Kingdom of God give us insight into who God is, how to approach him and what to ask him for, they teach us his ways and works, they show us the state of our souls and what we need to be working on in order to be ready for the Last Day, the great spiritual needs of the Church that we're part of and the larger world that still lies in darkness, and many other necessary insights. The more we learn, the more responsible we become, and the better job we can do with what God has called us to do.

Second, these truths give the church a standard system of beliefs that everyone can share. Unity comes first when everyone agrees – not necessarily with each other, but with what God says. If we learn from him, he will faithfully lead us into the truth that will unite us all. He doesn't teach his children contrary truths! If we believe something that is opposite from what our brother believes, then one of us isn't in touch with the Spirit and his leading. Someone is obviously getting something wrong when there's so much disagreement and fighting among us.

> Brothers, I could not address you as spiritual but as worldly — mere infants in Christ. I gave you milk, not solid food, for you were not yet ready for it. Indeed, you are still not ready. You are still worldly. For since there is jealousy and quarreling among you, are you not worldly? Are you not acting like mere men? (1 Corinthians 3:1-3)

If Christ's Church agrees on what the truth is, people from different individual churches can work together instead of against each other. Everyone shares the same truth, the same goals, the same methods – and all of us will be able to glorify the same God working among us.

Third, truth is the spring for a holy life. In the process of salvation, God first addresses our *minds* with the truth – he gives us knowledge, understanding and wisdom. Then when we are thinking straight, the Spirit moves that knowledge from our heads to our hearts – like a coffeepot percolating the coffee down to the cup.

> Be transformed by the renewing of your mind. Then you will be able to test and approve what God's will is — his good, pleasing and perfect will. (Romans 12:2)

Knowledge that stays in the head is useless; but the purpose of knowledge is to *change the heart.* Our emotions must measure up to God's standards of truth, because our emotions motivate us to live for God. Jesus said that we must "love the Lord our God with all our heart, mind and strength" and "love our neighbor as ourselves." In order to create and strengthen those emotions, we must first feed them with the Word of God.

A Catechism

The word "catechism" means "a form of instruction by means of questions and answers, particularly in the principles of religion." (Webster) It comes from the Greek word *katechismos*, which comes from the root word "to teach, instruct." From the times of the early Church, Christians have been taught the basics of the faith. For example, it was said that Apollos "had been instructed (*katechemenos*) in the way of the Lord." (Acts 18:25) Paul said that anyone receiving instruction (*katechoumenos*) in the Word must share all good things with his instructor (*katechounti*). (Galatians 6:6) Luke wrote his letter "so that you may know the certainly of the things you have been taught (*katechethes*)." (Luke 1:4)

The goal of the Church is to pass on her beliefs to the next generation.

> And the things you have heard me say in the presence of many witnesses entrust to reliable men who will also be qualified to teach others. (2 Timothy 2:2)

In doing this, the Church achieves two purposes: *first*, she preserves the truth as it stands in the Bible. Just the act of looking for the truth in God's Word and writing it down helps Christians know exactly what the truth is and the best way to say it. *This* is, in other words, what we believe as Christians – let the world make of it what it wants.

Second, the Church makes sure that the following generations hear the truth. Our children are our immediate responsibility before God. They will be charged to continue the work of the Church in their day, and it would be a shame if they had to discover God's truth all over again, starting at the beginning. It would be much better if we could give them the head-start they need to further the Kingdom, and not force them to retrace old ground to catch up.

The layout

The catechism that follows is meant for memorization and family study. Each lesson in the catechism has four parts:

The question: A question focuses the student's attention on a particular point of Christian truth. These questions cover the most important truths in our Christian faith. Notice that they follow the same order that standard works on theology and doctrine generally use.

The answer: The answer to the question is a short statement describing what the Bible teaches about a particular truth. It's designed to be easily memorized.

The passage: A passage from the Bible shows where this particular truth is taught. The student should be aware that this may not be the only place in the Bible where he can find the truth taught – he may find it taught in many other places as well. The idea is to get him started in his own Bible study.

The explanation: Finally, a short explanation follows that goes into some detail about the truth taught. The student doesn't need to memorize this part, but it would be helpful for him to know it well enough that he can put it in his own words when asked. The parents can help here.

Finally, there are pages for **Notes** following each section so that the student can record his own thoughts or study results.

The Bible

1) What is the Bible?

The Bible is the Word of God, the self-revelation of God.

> **These are the Scriptures that testify about me.** (*John 5:39*)

For a human soul, true life is spiritual life. In God we find our meaning, purpose, and only good. When we come into God's presence, therefore, we become alive spiritually. But since God is in Heaven and we are on earth, we need help to get in touch with him. The Bible brings God and man together. It uncovers the mystery behind God; it pulls away the veil and shows us what he's really like. It's the only truth about God that we can rely on. The Bible –

- keeps us from making up false gods (idolatry)
- tells us how to properly approach this God in prayer
- tells us *what* this God does and *how* he does it

And it's through the Bible that we communicate with God. The Spirit brings us into God's presence through the Word: there we hear him speak to us, and we find rebuke, comfort, encouragement and hope in his words to us. We also talk to him – in other words, pray – by means of the Bible: we desire and ask for what we read there. True prayer is based on our knowledge of God and his ways and works.

2) <u>What is the foundation of all of God's works?</u>

The Word of God is the foundation of all of God's works.

> In the beginning was the Word, and the Word was with God, and the Word was God. He was with God in the beginning. Through him all things were made; without him nothing was made that has been made. (John 1:3)

Whatever God does, he always does through his Word. For example, when God made the world, when Jesus raised the dead, when the Lord sent the people of Israel into exile – he first started by announcing what he would do, and explaining what people needed to know about his work.

These are the two things that the Word does for us. *First*, God reveals himself and his work to us. We wouldn't even know he was behind something if he didn't first tell us. In the Bible we can understand how he does things, and why he does things. The Bible is literally a window into God's spiritual world that helps us see what we would otherwise never see.

Second, the Word itself is God's will put to work. What God wants to do, he first announces. And whatever the edicts that the King pronounces has divine power to come to pass. The Word has power to create, change, destroy and recreate, as it issues from the mouth of God.

3) How are faith and the Bible related?

Faith comes from hearing the Word of God.

> Consequently, faith comes from hearing the message, and the message is heard through the word of Christ. (Romans 10:17)

The Bible opens up God's spiritual world so that we can see inside ¬ we can now know what God is really like, and what his ways and works are. We don't have to rely on man's vain imaginations about God any more.

But man's mind is closed to God, and to his revealing Word, until the Spirit of God opens it up with spiritual life. Without help from God, the Bible will be just another book that may be interesting but we won't get any salvation from it.

Faith is the spiritual skill that the Spirit gives us to understand the Bible. Faith is the ability to get past the words printed on the page to the world that it describes. Through our faith, the Spirit lifts us up into the presence of God, so that the God we heard about in the doctrine and history of the Bible suddenly becomes real to us.

Without faith, it is impossible to truly understand the Bible or come into God's presence to be saved. Faith and the Bible work hand in hand to make our God real to us.

4) What is truth?

The Bible is truth – it's the way God sees things.

> **Sanctify them by the truth; your Word is truth. (John 17:17)**

The Bible is the only truth about the subjects that it talks about. It's the standard that all human morals, actions, and knowledge must be based upon. It corrects our mistaken notions and guides us in correct thinking about God, ourselves, and the world we live in. Nothing else can be truth if it contradicts the Bible.

The reason that the Bible is the truth is because God is the author of the Bible. The Creator knows how he made the world, and therefore he knows what the truth is.

He caused the human authors to write his thoughts for us accurately, so that we can know for certain what those thoughts are. So the original Hebrew and Greek manuscripts that the Biblical authors themselves wrote were perfect and complete. Our Bibles today, since they are only translations, must strive to give us the meaning of those first manuscripts as best they can. But in God's Providence many translations that we have today give us the Word of God well enough that we can trust in them for our faith and practice.

5) How does the Bible help our worship?

The Bible tells us what to praise God for, and what to ask from him.

> One generation will commend your works to another; they will tell of your mighty acts. They will speak of the glorious splendor of your majesty, and I will meditate on your wonderful works. (Psalm 145:4-7)

Since we are obligated to worship God, and give him the glory he deserves, we need a certain amount of knowledge about God so that we can worship him acceptably. The Bible is a record of who God is, and what he has done. So, this written record is what we use when we –

- **Petition:** The Bible tells us what God did for his people in the past. This is recorded for *us,* so that now we know what to ask for – the same things he did for the saints of old. We have the same God as they had, and he works in the same ways; therefore we can be certain he will deal with us in the same way.

- **Worship:** The Bible tells us God's works, God's ways, and God's nature. We learn who he is through the Bible. We find out from this that we owe him everything, and that we were made only to serve him and make his amazing nature known to the world around us. Worship focuses our thoughts on God as described in his Word.

The books of the Bible

The Old Testament:

Genesis	2 Chronicles	Daniel
Exodus	Ezra	Hosea
Leviticus	Nehemiah	Joel
Numbers	Esther	Amos
Deuteronomy	Job	Obadiah
Joshua	Psalms	Jonah
Judges	Proverbs	Micah
Ruth	Ecclesiastes	Nahum
1 Samuel	Song of Songs	Habakkuk
2 Samuel	Isaiah	Zephaniah
1 Kings	Jeremiah	Haggai
2 Kings	Lamentations	Zechariah
1 Chronicles	Ezekiel	Malachi

The New Testament:

Matthew	Ephesians	Hebrews
Mark	Philippians	James
Luke	Colossians	1 Peter
John	1 Thessalonians	2 Peter
Acts	2 Thessalonians	1 John
Romans	1 Timothy	2 John
1 Corinthians	2 Timothy	3 John
2 Corinthians	Titus	Jude
Galatians	Philemon	Revelation

Notes

Notes

God

6) What is God?

God is Spirit.

> God is Spirit, and those who worship him
> must worship him in Spirit and in truth.
> (John 4:24)

God never had a beginning – he always has been, because nobody created him. He existed before anything in the universe existed. He doesn't need the universe in order to be fulfilled or complete. If he never created a thing outside of himself, he would be complete in himself and eternally satisfied.

God doesn't have a body like ours – he is pure Spirit. He can't be changed like we can – he is eternal and will never change. He is the original power, light, wisdom and majesty, from which all other things in the universe came. He is the source of all good things – which means the physical world depends on him, not the other way around. And God dwells in darkness, in mystery – which means that unless he reveals himself to us, we would never know what he is like.

So if we are to know God, we can't look at this world. The Spirit must take us outside the physical world and bring us into God's world of spirit. Whoever wants to know God must leave time and space behind and enter eternity, where there is only God.

7) What is the Trinity?

The Trinity is the Father, the Son, and the Holy Spirit – three persons, but one God.

> Who have been chosen according to the foreknowledge of God the Father, through the sanctifying work of the Spirit, for obedience to Jesus Christ and sprinkling by his blood. (1 Peter 1:2)

The word "Trinity" isn't found in the Bible, but the idea is there throughout the Bible. God is *one* God (Deuteronomy 6:4), but he's three Persons.

There's no denying that the Bible teaches about our Father who is God. The New Testament makes it very plain that Jesus Christ is the Son of God, a divine being who existed with the Father before the world was made. And the Spirit of God is obviously a person in himself who works on earth in a special role.

Where people go wrong about the Trinity is trying to explain how such a mystery could exist. But there are some things that we just have to accept without understanding them. When someone tries to explain how three Persons could be one God, they will inevitably say something wrong about him. Each person has a different "role" or relationship in the Godhead, but in the work of each person we see *one* God at work – not three Gods.

8) What does God need?

God needs nothing.

> And he is not served by human hands, as if he needed anything, because he himself gives all men life and breath and everything else.
> (Acts 17:25)

God is self-sufficient – which means that he doesn't need anything outside of himself. He needs nothing from us; he doesn't depend on his creation in any way at all. We could all suddenly cease to exist and he wouldn't change in the least.

This is important to believe because it shows that dependency only goes one way: we need God, not the other way around. If he gives us anything, it's simply out of his pure mercy and grace. He doesn't *have* to do anything for us. There is nothing we can do for God that would obligate him to us. He owes us nothing; our actions don't sway him in the least apart from his own will. We benefit tremendously from knowing God, whereas he gains nothing from us in the relationship. The creature, in other words, is totally dependent on the Creator, the servant on the King, and the redeemed on the Savior.

And that shows the depth of the love of God for his creatures – that even though he doesn't have to do anything for us, he still does it. This is why his mercy toward us is called "free grace."

9) What is the first thing that we will notice about God?

God is holy, holy, holy.

> **Holy, holy, holy is the LORD Almighty;**
> **the whole earth is full of his glory.**
> **(Isaiah 6:3)**

When the Bible says that God is holy, it means several things: *first*, that God is special. He is goodness, righteousness, wisdom and power. He is perfect in himself – he needs nothing else to be complete. Nobody else is like God – he is unique.

That fact is proved when all his creatures depend on God for their very existence. He literally is their life, their well-being, their entire purpose for existing. He is like the hub of a wheel: we are all connected to him because we can't exist without him. He made us that way – if we could separate ourselves from him we would immediately die.

This brings us to the *second* meaning of holiness: there's an aura around him that strikes us with fear, respect and worship whenever we see him. We *know*, as soon as we get a look at him, just how unique he is and how completely we are in his hands. We know that we exist only because he willed it so. And what put fear in Isaiah's heart when he saw this God was that he was separated from this God because of his sin, and normally that means instant death. There can be no life apart from God, and he requires righteousness if we want to continue living. Someday we are all going to give an account of why we had so little to do with a God who continually holds us in his hand.

10) What is God's special name?

God's special name is Yahweh.

> The LORD, the LORD, the compassionate and gracious God, slow to anger, abounding in love and faithfulness, maintaining love to thousands, and forgiving wickedness, rebellion and sin. Yet he does not leave the guilty unpunished; he punishes the children and their children for the sin of the fathers to the third and fourth generation. (Exodus 34:6-7)

Israel's God is unique – and this name shows what he's really like. No other religion has a God like the LORD.

The Hebrew word for the English translation "LORD" is **Yahweh**. As we read here in Exodus, Yahweh is a God who saves sinners from their sin. He is not only open to the idea, he longs to save us! No other God is so longsuffering with sinners, and so amazingly willing to redeem people who don't deserve forgiveness.

Israel found out many times that it was a mercy to have this God. In spite of their many sins and failings, he continually delivered them from their problems and restored them to fellowship with him. When Jesus came later, the Jews again experienced the deep love of their God as he offered his only Son for their sins, according to the definition of his special name. But in order to get deliverance from Yahweh, they had to call on that Name in faith – see Joel 2:32. Only when they turned to *that* God would they get forgiveness.

The Name Yahweh

Exodus 34:6-7 is the Lord's definition of his own Name. Whatever people make of the Hebrew name, this is what God wanted the Israelites to call on him for.

The Hebrew name is יהוה (or YHWH), which is known as the Tetragrammaton in Jewish circles. Since the Jews didn't write vowels in their words at first, nobody knows to this day how to pronounce this special Name – a real pity, since the Jews were commanded to call on him by Name!

English translations render the Name in different ways. Sometimes you will see it translated as **Jehovah** (KJV). In most versions you will see **LORD** (with all capital letters – it's not the same as **Lord**, which is another Hebrew word). Sometimes you will find the word **Yahweh**, which is a modern attempt at fitting vowels between the consonants.

The name Jesus comes from this special name. **Jesus** ('Ιησοῦς) is the Greek form of the Hebrew name **Yahoshua** (יְהוֹשֻׁעַ), which is the proper name **Joshua**. In other words, Joshua would have been called "Jesus" had he lived in New Testament times. The name Jesus is a combination of two Hebrew words:

> **Ya** – a short form of Yahweh
> **Hoshua** – salvation
>
> **Jesus** = *Yahweh is salvation*

So the Son of God came with the name of the Old Testament God – he was ready to do what his ancient name promised.

The attributes of God

God has certain attributes, or characteristics, that tell us what he's like.

<u>Spiritual</u> (he is not physical, nor is he part of his creation)

<u>Eternal</u> (he has no beginning and no end)

<u>Immutable</u> (he never changes)

<u>Omnipresent</u> (he is present everywhere)

<u>Omniscient</u> (he knows all things)

<u>Almighty</u> (he has infinite power)

<u>Holy</u> (he is the only good, and perfect)

<u>Good</u> (he cares for all of his creatures)

<u>Wise</u> (his works are perfect and accomplish his purposes)

<u>Just</u> (he judges accurately, and his rewards and punishments are fitting and appropriate)

<u>Merciful and gracious</u> (he extends love and forgiveness freely to those who don't deserve them)

<u>Longsuffering</u> (he is not easily provoked, and forgives sinners repeatedly)

<u>Patient</u> (he works over time)

The Ways of the Lord

> **And if you walk in my ways and obey my statutes and commands as David your father did, I will give you a long life. (1 Kings 3:14)**

God has ways of doing things. His ways are not our ways, and they aren't the way we like to do things. But his ways work: following his ways means life for us. If we learn what his ways are, and work along with him instead of against him, his ways lead us to Heaven.

He works through his little children – they are his special servants through whom God is building his eternal Kingdom.

He uses faith to do the big jobs – faith lays hold of a God who does the impossible – it gives God the opportunity to do miracles.

He uses time to ripen – God always develops his plans over time, so that all the pieces will come together at the right time.

He uses a little to accomplish a lot – God doesn't need much to work with – he delights in using just a little to show his miraculous power.

He builds up instead of tears down – God is the Creator, not the destroyer – he is building an eternal Kingdom to replace the one we ruined.

He works through his Spirit – The Spirit of God is the power behind all of God's works.

He wins by losing – God often will bring someone through loss or failure to show his power to pull victory out of defeat.

He uses man to do his work – Though he could do everything himself, God chose to make man a co-laborer in the building of the Kingdom – and therefore responsible for the outcome.

The Works of the Lord

The works of the Lord will tell us a great deal about what our God is like. We need to know what God's works are because they tell us what kind of God he is. Watching him in action does many things that are important for us: it teaches us the truth about him, it increases our faith in him, it teaches us what to expect from him, it warns us not to try such things ourselves, and it teaches us to wait on him to do his special work in our lives.

We need to focus on God's works for a change. All we seem to hear about these days are man's works, and what man can do. There is no help in man! The good news of the Gospel is the special work that only God can do for the human heart. There, in his work, is our salvation and hope.

The seven works of God

Creation and Providence

The Making of Israel

Judgment

The Coming of Christ

Building up a Kingdom

The Last Day

Scripture

Notes

Creation

11) What did God use to make the world?

God made the world out of nothing.

> By faith we understand that the universe was formed at God's command, so that what is seen was not made out of what was visible.
> (Hebrews 11:3)

God created the world out of nothing – which means he didn't use a physical process that man could understand. He skipped the steps between his will and its fulfillment – what he wanted, suddenly came to be.

Since nothing existed in the beginning except God himself, of course he would have had to create matter and energy out of nothing! The Bible says that "the earth was formless and empty" (Genesis 1:2). That's another way of saying that nothing existed: matter as we know it has three dimensions (form) and it is solid, not empty (void). So this was a Hebraism for saying that nothing existed at the beginning.

The universe had a definite beginning, before which time it didn't exist. What's important about this is that God isn't the same as his creation. He isn't one with it; he existed before the world did, and the world isn't eternal like God is. He exists completely apart from his creation, and he doesn't change in response to whatever his creation undergoes.

The world had nothing to do with its own creation – it depends completely on God for its continued existence.

12) How did God make the world?

God made the world by miracles.

> By the word of the LORD were the heavens made, their starry host by the breath of his mouth. (Psalm 33:6)

A miracle is something that God does with his own hand, apart from natural means. Man can't understand a miracle because we need to see the steps between the start of a project and its completion in order to understand it. But when God works, he doesn't use intermediary steps as we would. He simply speaks, and what he wants appears out of nowhere.

For example, to make bread, we go through the necessary steps between sowing the seed and baking the bread. But God makes bread out of nothing: witness his work in the desert for the Israelites, providing them with manna out of the sky. Jesus did the same thing when he fed thousands of people at one time.

The miracle of creation is the model for rest of God's works that are recorded in the Bible. We learn from Genesis that God *prefers* to use miracles to do his work. It's necessary that he does so – otherwise it would never happen on its own! The world can't make itself, nor can it hold itself together or give itself meaning and purpose. God alone must do these things for the world.

13) What are the two parts of creation?

The creation is spiritual and physical.

> **Do you not know that your body is a temple of the Holy Spirit, who is in you, whom you have received from God? (1 Corinthians 6:19)**

God made a universe that's made up of physical and spiritual realities. We can understand the physical side of the world because our senses tell us what it's like. But that's only one side of the universe.

He made the soul of man, for example, that is capable of knowing and communicating with God. He made Heaven, man's eternal home after this world is destroyed. He also made Hell, which will be the eternal punishment for sinners. He designed the world in such a way that it responds to man's moral works. That is, as we do right, the creation prospers; as we do wrong, the creation suffers.

The physical and spiritual sides of Creation are tightly integrated so that it achieves both our goals and God's goals. On Judgment Day we will be judged by our works "done while in the body" – we will then realize, if we didn't know it before, that our lives were actually a stage, so to speak, in which we acted out our parts and formed our eternal destiny.

This is why questions of right and wrong are extremely important – the destiny of our souls depends on what we do in our bodies.

14) What did God call the world he had made?

God called his world very good.

> **God saw all that he had made, and it was very good. (Genesis 1:31)**

God made the world "very good" – which means that it was exactly what he wanted it to be. His world was perfect; it was a balanced creation in which each part played an important role that the rest of the universe depended on. Everything was placed and made in such a way that the world was an entire picture, able to grow and develop over time. Yet each part fit into the picture with such precision that, if you would remove it, it would mean endangering the entire structure.

Man could not improve it. Man's responsibility was to *maintain* that original creation. He was made ruler over God's works in order to glorify God – meaning that God's original purpose and design in the way he made the world was all-important and must not be changed, only maintained.

When man changed the world to suit himself – after his fall into sin – he actually turned his back on what God called "very good" and tried to remake the world to be something "better." The result was disaster, a ruined kingdom. Man can't improve on God's original design.

15) <u>Through whom did God make the world?</u>

God made the world through Christ.

> **For by him all things were created: things in heaven and on earth, visible and invisible, whether thrones or powers or rulers or authorities; all things were created by him and for him. (Colossians 1:16)**

Jesus Christ is the "project manager," so to speak, of Creation. God created the world through him for several reasons: *first*, the entire universe was designed to be subject to him. He is the King of kings, the Master of the world that every created thing serves. He has complete control over everything so that he can direct its course toward his own goals. This world belongs to Christ, and exists to serve and please him alone.

Second, he had long-range plans at creation – he wanted to do more than just set up the physical universe. He knew that sin would ruin the first creation, so he started laying the groundwork (at the beginning) for fixing the lawlessness that the world would fall into. In other words, in order to start working on a new Creation, he had to have complete control over the first one. The new creation was to be sinless, perfect, and eternal. In order to achieve that, Christ had to have full authority and power over the first creation to bend it to his will.

So, in this physical world Christ lays the foundation of the spiritual world that will eventually replace the first creation. The Savior *has* to be the Creator, so that everything to work out in the end the way he wants it.

16) What is Providence?

Providence is God's continual care for his creatures.

> **The eyes of all look to you, and you give them their food at the proper time. You open your hand and satisfy the desires of every living thing. (Psalm 145:15-16)**

God made the world through miracles, but he made the world to keep running according to unchanging laws that science can understand and describe to us. We can use these scientific principles to make our lives more comfortable and prosperous.

However, God wisely designed the world in such a way that he himself provides for our daily needs. It's no accident that there is always food to eat, air to breathe, and plenty of materials on hand for us to work with. Though we often don't give him credit for creating our world to be a comfort and source of supply for us, it's true nevertheless. Scientists can tell us the physical laws that make our world work, but their instruments can't show us that God's hand monitors the system continuously.

We ought not to take all this careful planning and support for granted. If he wished, he could remove his hand and his creatures would suffer and die as a result. We are so dependent on him for even the simplest things in life that we truly are children compared to him, even the strongest and wisest of us. And we should also realize that he cares and provides for us for a reason: he is giving us the necessities of life so that we can be free to pursue even more important issues – that is, building the Kingdom of God.

Notes

Notes

Man

17) How is man different from the rest of Creation?

Man was made in the image of God.

> So God created man in his own image, in the image of God he created him. (Genesis 1:27)

God breathed into man and man became "a living being." (Genesis 2:7) Man alone has a spirit in him; that's what gives him the "image of God." Animals, though the Scriptures also call them "living creatures," don't have a spirit in them connecting them with God.

The spirit of man enables him to walk in the presence of God, even while he walks here on earth. Man was made to be aware of God's world as much as he was aware of his physical surroundings.

One of the meanings behind the word "image" is that man has the ability to communicate with God. Since man has an important part to play in God's creation, it's necessary that he be able to hear God, understand his Word, and carry out God's instructions to do his job.

And because man was made in God's image, he is like a living reminder of God to the rest of Creation. The world would feel the hand of God, and be guided in God's will, by means of the work of man. Man represented God on earth in order to build God's Kingdom.

18) How does man resemble the Trinity?

God made man to be male and female.

> **Male and female he created them.**
> **(Genesis 1:27)**

God made man "male and female" – which means that *family* is the foundation of all levels of human society. Of course, the fact that they are male and female doesn't explain why they are like the Trinity, because even animals were created male and female. But man is the *ruler* over Creation. And in order to carry out their responsibilities in life, people need to work with each other. In the family, each person has his or her own job to do, and all are under authority.

The passage actually says that "in the image of God he created him; male and female he created them." (Genesis 1:27) The wording here shows that *relationship* is the root idea of "the image of God."

The Trinity – which is the Father, Son and Holy Spirit – are *one* with each other, and they constantly fellowship with each other. (John 17:21-23) Man was made to do the same thing in his family: man and woman would become one (Genesis 2:24), and along with their children would become a "trinity" – three parts making one whole. Each person brings his/her own skills and characteristics to the relationship; each one contributes what they can do in order to reach their goals. Through love for each other, and cooperation and working together, the result is a world of blessing, balance, and peace as the Creator intended.

19) What job did God give to man?

God made man to be the ruler over God's creation.

> God blessed them and said to them, "Be fruitful and increase in number; fill the earth and subdue it. Rule over the fish of the sea and the birds of the air and over every living creature that moves on the ground." (Genesis 1:28)

God made a Kingdom when he made the world. It is full of his creatures, all made to serve him. He set everything up in the world in such a way that each creature, each rock and tree and star, has its own part to play to form a complete, balanced world in which nothing is missing and everything depends on everything else.

God of course is the King over all, but he assigned man the job of being his co-ruler under him. Man is the contact point between God and the world. He is God's representative on earth: through him, the world will be ruled by God's Law and will experience God's blessings.

Through his mind (which is able to understand God's Laws), and his spirit (through which he can walk in the presence of God), man can successfully govern the earth and maintain the original balance and blessing that God first created.

20) What is man's created nature?

Man was made upright.

> **This only have I found: God made mankind upright, but men have gone in search of many schemes. (Ecclesiastes 7:29)**

God is righteous. And since man was made in God's image, that means that man is to be righteous too. God can't abide sin and rebellion, and he expects his kingdom to serve him in holiness and righteousness in all things.

"Holiness" on earth means this: to be set apart for God's use. The articles in the Temple of the Old Testament were "sanctified," or "made holy" (it's the same word in the original language) by assigning them to be used only in the service of God. It was forbidden to use them for any secular purpose after they had been made holy.

In the same way, man was God's special servant – he was set apart for God's work, not his own. The reason is obvious. If man is to be the ruler under God over the world, his role is critical to the success of God's Kingdom. He must devote his entire life to his calling. He's the keystone that holds the entire arch of Creation together. As long as he remains righteous and devoted to God's Kingdom, the entire creation will prosper. But if man himself rebels against God's Law, the entire world would immediately fall into death, misery and destruction. Wherever man leads, the world that God made for him to rule over will follow him.

21) What is man's purpose?

Man was made to glorify God and enjoy him forever.

> **So whether you eat or drink or whatever you do, do it all for the glory of God.**
> **(1 Corinthians 10:31)**

Giving God glory means giving him credit for what he deserves. Man's job on earth, therefore, is to focus attention on God – the Creator, the giver of all good things, the King who rules over his Kingdom, and the Redeemer.

God deserves all glory. Everything that happens in his world depends on him alone. He gives us food, shelter, protection, love and mercy, forgiveness, and hope for the future. He gives us meaning and purpose in life. If God would take away his Spirit, we would all return back to the dust we came from. Every one of us literally depend on him daily for life and breath.

The world must know this – God must get credit for what he does. So many people think that the world runs on its own, and man must look to himself for what he needs. So our calling in life is to direct everyone's attention to the only God, so that they will return to depend on him for everything – as they were created to do.

Notes

The Law

22) What does the Law show us about God?

The Law describes what God calls righteous.

> So then, the law is holy, and the commandment is holy, righteous and good.
> (Romans 7:12)

God is righteous, and his Law describes to us what "righteousness" means to God. We don't have to guess what is right and wrong in God's eyes. The Law tells us plainly what his standards are.

And since God made a Kingdom, and since he's the King, we shouldn't be surprised that he alone lays down the rules and laws of that Kingdom which he expects everyone to obey.

These laws are what makes for a happy and prosperous Kingdom. When we follow that Law, we discover that it's the best possible way to run a kingdom. Everyone benefits when we all obey God's Law. Everyone prospers, everyone is able to live with others and please God, everyone has purpose and meaning in life.

God does all things well, because it's in his nature to be good to his creatures and take care of their every need. The Law shows us his infinite goodness and his unfailing wisdom in how he governs over his Creation.

23) What does the Law describe?

The Law describes a perfect man.

> **Blessed are they whose ways are blameless, who walk according to the Law of the LORD. (Psalm 119:1)**

Anybody who wishes to please God must keep his Law perfectly. Not only is God righteous, but he expects everything and everyone around him to be holy and righteous as well. He has that right, as the builder and master of his own house. In order to live with God, we must measure up to his standards of what is holy and right.

Adam and Eve were made holy, though they fell into sin later. And the Law describes where they went wrong. If they had remained in their state of holiness, all of their children – including us – would be morally perfect according to the Law.

But since sin entered into the human race and infected everyone, only Jesus has achieved this high level of righteousness. If we compare his life with the demands of the Law, we can see clearly how he "fulfilled all righteousness" by keeping the Law to the letter, and according to its spirit. When God announced that his Son was pleasing to him (Matthew 3:17), he was saying that here was a man who fit the description of a perfect person, according to the Law.

24) <u>How do we know what sin is?</u>

The Law of God tells us what sin is.

> What shall we say, then? Is the law sin?
> Certainly not! Indeed I would not have
> known what sin was except through the law.
> For I would not have known what coveting
> really was if the law had not said, "Do not
> covet." (Romans 7:7)

God tells us specifically in his Law what he wants us to live like in his Kingdom. It includes not only outward actions but the thoughts and emotions of the heart. It covers all aspects of living with God and with his people. Since it's God's Kingdom that we live in, and God himself is the King and Judge, we aren't free to decide for ourselves what sin is. The Law is always the standard for sin and righteousness.

Sin is rebellion against God's Law. (1 John 3:4) When someone breaks the Law of God, what he's actually doing is putting the Creation and its peace and prosperity into jeopardy. It's the same thing as a traitor who turns his back on his country and commits acts that endanger the other citizens.

This is why God takes sin so seriously – it's a crime of treachery and disloyalty against his Kingdom. The King has to be tough with sinners, because if they go unchecked then a lot of people will hurt as a result, and God's eternal goals won't be fulfilled.

25) How far does the Law reach?

The Law reaches into our hearts.

> **We know that the law is spiritual; but I am unspiritual, sold as a slave to sin. (Romans 7:14)**

The Law of God isn't just a matter of following rules for outward behavior. God is interested in the heart, because it's out of the heart that we show what we really are. Jesus said that "out of the heart come evil thoughts, murder, adultery, sexual immorality, theft, false testimony, slander." (Matthew 15:19)

Our hearts direct our lives: we are creatures of love and hate, peace and war, gentleness and harshness, and many other emotions that guide our actions. In order to fully govern a person's actions, therefore, the Law itself must reach into the depths of the heart – it must deal with spiritual issues.

When Jesus taught his disciples on the mountain (Matthew 5-7), he showed them the true depth of the Law. Jesus didn't contradict the Law, or make up a new Law and set aside the old one. People may want to be hypocrites and hide what's in their hearts with good works, but God will never be deceived by them. The Law, according to him, always did have a spiritual depth to it that convicts sinners of what is in their hearts.

26) What does the Law to do sinners?

The Law condemns sinners.

> All who rely on observing the law are under a curse, for it is written: "Cursed is everyone who does not continue to do everything written in the Book of the Law." (Galatians 3:10)

We are all sinners, by God's definition, and therefore all of us are under a curse of death. Adam and Eve first plunged the human race into this situation, and we are all born into it with no hope of escaping it.

There is such an amazing depth and scope to God's Law that we *will* break some aspect of it during our lifetimes, no matter how hard we try not to. The Law covers things that we ought to do, and things that we ought not to do; it covers spiritual and heart issues as well as outward acts. It covers our relationship with God as well as with our fellow man. And the Law is what *God* considers righteousness, not the changing opinions of men in various cultures. The Law is so complex that there's simply no way that a person can keep the entire Law to perfection and please an infinitely holy God.

The Law is *not* the sinner's friend! Too many people think that they can keep some of the Law and please God as a result. They don't realize that they're *already* in trouble with the Law. On Judgment day, if they are found guilty of breaking only one of the laws, they will be judged as "law-breakers" (James 2:10-11) and punished accordingly – no matter what else they might have done right.

Notes

Sin

27) What is sin?

Sin is lawlessness.

> **Everyone who sins breaks the Law; in fact, sin is lawlessness. (1 John 3:4)**

Sin is rebellion against God's Law. God made man to be the ruler over Creation, and man's first responsibility was to make sure that the Law of God would be upheld and enforced throughout the world. But when Adam and Eve led the human race into sin, we all became rebels against God. Now we have little or no interest in doing what God expects of us.

Many people define sin in many ways, and usually they define it in such a way as to make it easy to cure if they want to. For example, some people think sin is selfishness – so to be righteous, according to them, all we have to do is be more generous to others.

But since sin is rebellion against God, it's not nearly so easy to fix. We've already broken his laws, and now we have to pay the penalty. In a court of law, the judge isn't impressed with our intentions to do better in the future. If we've been convicted of a crime, we must first pay the penalty for that past act.

Rebellion is an act of treachery against the King; it's not a small matter. Traitors are usually shot, because their crime put the lives and peace of the country in jeopardy. Sin requires a severe penalty from a just Judge – usually death. In other words, since we are now guilty of sin, there's nothing we can do to fix things. God must make the next move. Either he punishes us, or he finds some way to clear us of guilt. But either way we are at his mercy.

28) What is the punishment for sin?

The punishment for sin is death.

> The wages of sin is death. (Romans 6:23)

Sin is actually treachery against the King, a crime against the Kingdom of God. Man was created to be vice-regent under God, responsible for the well-being of the Kingdom of God on earth. When he rebelled against God, therefore, it was a greater tragedy than we can possibly imagine.

Traitors against the state are usually executed. They put the lives of their fellow citizens in jeopardy by their crimes. They invited the enemy inside the borders, or sold state secrets to the enemy. Such a crime can't go unpunished, and its penalty must be the supreme punishment.

When God doomed Adam and Eve to death for their rebellion, it was a fitting punishment. Consider that they threw all of their descendants into the same rebellious nature, and opened the way for our great Enemy on earth, and you can see that the damage done to humanity was staggering. Now we are all born into sin, we can't help but sin against God, and we actually prefer sin to God's commands.

Physical death is only the first step of the punishment against sin. God denied Adam the right to the Tree of Life, because he didn't want man to live forever in sin. But the soul of man is also dead, which means that our contact with God is broken. We can't know God, or be in communication with God, as man was first intended to be.

29) How many people are sinners?

Every human being, except for Jesus Christ, is a sinner.

> Therefore, just as sin entered the world through one man, and death through sin, and in this way death came to all men, because all sinned ... (Romans 5:12-14)

Adam and Eve died spiritually in the day they ate of the forbidden fruit of the Tree of the Knowledge of Good and Evil. That means that all of their physical descendants, except for Jesus Christ, are also rebellious sinners against God. We are all born into sin.

We certainly didn't ask to be born sinners, but this doesn't excuse us from God's wrath against sinners. We actually prefer our sin to God's righteous commands. Give a person a chance, and he or she would prefer his own sin to the Law's righteousness. We are all like that, even from childhood.

Not every person has broken *every* command in the Law. But judgment against us doesn't depend on that. If we've broken only one Law, that brands us as traitors and Law-breakers. (1 John 3:4) But it's not necessary to prove that we've broken *all* of the laws. We are sinners because we are naturally rebellious at heart, and we've proven many times in the circumstances of our own lives that we don't want to do things God's way.

30) What can we do about our sin?

We can do nothing about our sin.

> **We know that the law is spiritual; but I am unspiritual, sold as a slave to sin.**
> **(Romans 7:14)**

Our crime against God is that we have broken his Law; so God is the only one now who can do anything about our sin.

We are in the same situation as a criminal in a courtroom. The criminal must be brought before the judge, and the judge must review the facts to determine what really happened. The court isn't free to release the criminal simply because he promises to do better in the future! The court's job is to administer justice, therefore there *must* be a judgment and a sentence for the crime committed.

What we've done against God can't be changed now. It's in the past, and we can only wait for judgment. God fully intends to review the case of every human being, because justice demands that our crimes against his Kingdom be brought to light and punished. If there is to be mercy, that will be up to him – but it must come *after* the judgment of "guilty."

Since there is a way to escape the sentence of eternal death, we do have hope – but our hope should never be in trying to make ourselves better or impressing God with our good works. It's a foregone conclusion that God will declare us to be sinners; our hope lies only in the good works of another, not in ours. Salvation rests on what Jesus does for us, not in what we do for ourselves.

31) What is the final end of sinners?

God will deliver all unrepentant sinners to Hell on the Last Day.

> If anyone's name was not found written in the book of life, he was thrown into the lake of fire. (Revelation 20:15)

When Adam sinned, his soul died and he lost contact with the Creator. And his body started the process of dying, eventually turning to the dust he came from. Now all of his children experience both kinds of death – physical and spiritual.

But the tragedy isn't over yet. Those people who lived their entire lives in rebellion against their Creator, and would have nothing to do with their Redeemer, will be "thrown outside, into the darkness, where there will be weeping and gnashing of teeth." (Matthew 8:12) God reacts in terrible anger to traitors against his Kingdom and his Law.

Hell is eternal separation from God and the misery that comes from that separation. It's also a never-ending torment that results from God's wrath. What people don't realize is how devastating that experience will be. Life in this world is full of God's blessings, showered daily even on those who live in rebellion against him. Hell, however, will be the end of those undeserved blessings and the beginning of eternal destruction.

But there will be no injustice in putting souls in Hell, because deep in the hearts of sinners they would prefer any amount of misery to bowing in submission to God and serving the King.

Notes

The Covenant

32) What does the word "covenant" mean?

Covenant means "to cut an agreement."

> Abram brought all these to him, cut them in two and arranged the halves opposite each other; the birds, however, he did not cut in half. (Genesis 15:10)

The word "covenant" in the Old Testament usually appears with another Hebrew word that means "to cut." It was a way that two people could make a serious agreement with each other and make sure that each one would fulfill his side of the bargain.

They would take some animals and cut them into halves, and lay the halves out on the ground in two rows. Then each person would walk down between the halves and state what he promised to do in the agreement. The ceremony symbolized the startling fact that if one of the parties failed to keep his side of the bargain, the other party would have the right to cut him in half with a sword just as they did to the animals!

This is precisely the kind of agreement that God made with Abraham and his heirs – you can read the story in Genesis 15. It shows how seriously God took his promises to Abraham. But notice that God didn't require Abraham to walk between the animals; this is because he knew that Abraham and his heirs would sin and break the covenant, and God didn't want the covenant to be jeopardized. So he himself decided to keep the entire covenant for both sides.

33) To whom was the covenant made?

The covenant was made to Abraham and his Seed.

> The promises were spoken to Abraham and to his seed. The Scripture does not say "and to seeds," meaning many people, but "and to your seed," meaning one person, who is Christ. (Galatians 3:16)

God made the covenant with Abraham and his heirs. At first the Jews thought that this meant only them, since they are the direct physical descendants of Abraham. But in the New Testament we find out that a person is a descendant of Abraham – and therefore a legal heir of the covenant – if he has the *spiritual* characteristics of his forefather.

First, the promise was made to Abraham and his seed. Paul points out here in this passage that the word used is "Seed," not "seeds." The difference is critical. Obviously God had in mind that Jesus Christ is the fulfillment of the covenant; every part of the covenant finds its complete form in the person and work of Christ. He himself will fulfill the covenant for God's people; and whoever is part of him, will have it all. (Galatians 3:29)

Second, God specifically pointed out what the family characteristic is: **faith**. And it's not just any kind of faith – it has to be the same kind that Abraham learned about. See Romans 4 for a description of this special faith. Whoever has Abraham's faith is a child of Abraham and therefore rightful heir of the covenant. (Romans 4:16)

34) What are the four points of the covenant?

The promise of the son. (Genesis 15:2-4) God promised to give Abraham a son by means of a miracle. Abraham, and especially his wife Sarah, were too old to have children. But unless he had a son there would be no heir of his estate. God gave him Isaac after 25 years of waiting. The son would be the means of continuing the family line and preserving the covenant.

The promise of the land. (Genesis 13:14) God promised to give the land of Canaan to Abraham, and especially to his heirs. At first this seemed to be impossible too, since the Canaanites weren't about to hand over their valuable property to an alien shepherd! But through the death of Sarah, Abraham got a legal deed and title to a portion of the land that the family would later return and redeem.

The promise of the nation. (Genesis 12:2) Often a family had no means of knowing whether they would survive, since life was extremely dangerous in those days with disease, bandits and roving armies destroying whole towns. But God promised to multiply Abraham's descendants into a great nation – the Jews, who have been around for 4000 years! The fulfillment first came when God led Rebekah (miraculously) to agree to be Isaac's wife, the necessary first step to building a family line.

The promise of the blessing. (Genesis 12:3) The curse of mankind is death, due to our sins. So the blessing to all nations would be the reversal of death – resurrection from the dead. Abraham first tasted this promise when he received his son Isaac back from the dead, spared from sacrifice.

35) What is the spiritual covenant?

The promise of the son – <u>Jesus</u>. The real son that God had in mind was Jesus Christ. He also was a miracle baby – born to Mary without a human father. In him the entire covenant is contained and fulfilled; he is the heir through whom the rest of us will become heirs. If we are spiritually one with Christ, then we will receive the same promises that were made to Abraham.

The promise of the land – <u>Heaven</u>. The land that God had in mind to give his people is Heaven, a place where there will be eternal joy and peace. Canaan was a symbol of a greater spiritual place of rest that the entire Church is to enjoy. Even the saints of old knew that the promise that God made them was not part of this fallen, temporary world.

The promise of the nation – <u>the Church</u>. The Jews are the physical descendants of Abraham, but God had in mind a much larger nation consisting not only of Jews but of Gentiles as well. The promise would extend to all who had the faith of Abraham, over the entire world and throughout time.

The promise of the blessing – <u>resurrection from the dead</u>. This too has a spiritual fulfillment, since receiving eternal *physical* life would be somewhat of a let-down in light of what God has in store for us in Heaven. His saints will be raised on the last day with *spiritual* bodies, capable of enjoying God directly forever, without possibility of corruption from sin and death.

36) Who are the heirs of the covenant to Abraham?

All who are in Christ are heirs of the covenant to Abraham.

> **If you belong to Christ, then you are Abraham's seed, and heirs according to the promise. (Galatians 3:29)**

To the Jews, genealogy was everything. Every Jew had to prove through family records that he was a physical descendant of Abraham – if he or she wanted any of the covenant blessings. If someone couldn't prove his family ancestry, he was put out of the covenant community.

The spiritual covenant that God made with Abraham is also exclusive. God can't give it to just anybody; he himself must stick to the terms of the original agreement and bless only the children of Abraham. If he broke these terms and gave it out to non-children, he would be liable to death at Abraham's hand! (See Genesis 15:8-21)

But instead of proving that one is physically descended from Abraham, Christians have a spiritual characteristic in their hearts that proves that they are his children: Abraham's faith. When God sees that in us, he considers us heirs of the covenant, and he can legally bless us with it. But we also know that only those people who are in Christ have this faith; it's a gift from God when we are first converted.

For an excellent example of Jesus keeping the legal terms of the covenant – and only handing it out when he sees faith – study the story in Matthew 15:21-28.

Notes

Jesus Christ

37) Who is the Father of Jesus?

God is the Father of Jesus.

> **And a voice from Heaven said, "This is my Son, whom I love; with him I am well pleased." (Matthew 3:17)**

God is one God, but he is three persons – and Jesus is one of those persons of the Godhead. He is called the "only-begotten" son of the Father – which means that he alone *comes from* the Father, and shares the Father's divine nature as God. All of God's other "sons" are adopted.

Jesus existed from before Creation as the Son of God. He always has been, and has never himself been created – in fact, he himself is the Creator!

Since he is fully divine, becoming a man on earth didn't change his divine nature in the least. When he took on human form, it was God coming into the flesh – which is why he was given the name Immanuel, "God with us."

The incarnation of Christ was a miracle because the child Jesus was conceived in Mary by the Holy Spirit, not by the act of Joseph. Christ's Father in Heaven made it very plain that this person was God's Son, not man's, at his baptism and in various ways during his ministry.

The point is important because we have to know *where he came from* – from God in Heaven, not from earth – and *what he is doing here* – God's work, not man's.

38) What does the book of Ruth teach us about Christ?

Christ is our Redeemer.

> He redeemed us in order that the blessing
> given to Abraham might come to the Gentiles
> through Christ Jesus, so that by faith we
> might receive the promise of the Spirit.
> (Galatians 3:14)

The story of Ruth teaches us several things about the way Jesus saves us. *First*, Ruth was an alien, an outsider to the Israelite nation. She had no claim on the covenant of Abraham. *Second*, she was a Moabite, which the Law had laid a curse upon. Because of the way the Moabites had treated the Israelites in the desert, no Moabite was allowed in Israel down to the tenth generation (See Deuteronomy 23:3-6). But by the law of redemption, a man could buy the property of a deceased Israelite and marry his widow, in order to save the inheritance. That's what Boaz did, but he did it not for the Law's sake but because he loved Ruth.

We are in the same predicament. Being Gentiles, none of us have a legal right to the Abrahamic Covenant. Plus, being sinners, we are under the curse of the Law. But Jesus the Redeemer purchased us through his death, and now we belong to him. He saved us from the curse of the Law (Galatians 3:13), brought us into the community of faith, all for his love for us – the love of a husband. See Ephesians 5:25-27 and Revelation 19:7-9 for the marriage of Christ with the Church.

39) How is Jesus related to man?

Jesus is the Son of Man.

> In the future you will see the Son of Man
> sitting at the right hand of the Mighty One
> and coming on the clouds of heaven.
> (Matthew 26:64)

Jesus was born a real human being. He put aside his glory (but not his divinity – he remained the Son of God even as he became a man) and took on a human body. He was born to the virgin Mary by the action of the Holy Spirit.

Though he had no earthly father (his birth was a miracle) he was fully human. He had all the characteristics of a man except sin. He retained all the characteristics as the second person of the Trinity except the glory that he had with his Father before his physical birth. He was both God and man in one person.

The reason he became a man was because, by God's decree, a man had to fulfill all righteousness according to the Law. A man had to suffer under the penalty of the Law and die for sin. And a man had to ascend to the throne of Heaven so that the rest of us would have the right to go there later. If the rest of us are to have anything from God, the man Jesus had to blaze the way first and please God in everything that he did.

40) What kind of man was Jesus?

Jesus was a sinless man.

> For we do not have a high priest who is unable to sympathize with our weaknesses, but we have one who has been tempted in every way, just as we are — yet was without sin. (Hebrews 4:15)

The Law of God describes what a perfect person should be like. It describes the things that a man should do, and the things he shouldn't do, if he wants to please a holy God.

Jesus fulfilled the Law perfectly as a man. Everything he did was pleasing to God. Not only did he live a perfectly righteous life – so much so that the Law has no problem with his moral character – he also took on himself all the punishment that the Law dictates against sinners. He fulfilled the sacrificial laws to the letter, so that all who come to Jesus to be saved will find that everything necessary to save them has already been taken care of.

The Law has a spiritual depth to it, as well as an outward physical aspect. Jesus gave us an idea of that depth when he taught us some of the deeper aspects of the Law in the Sermon on the Mount. The Law requires righteousness *of the heart*, not just of the hands and feet. And in his heart, Jesus was the perfection of what God had in mind when he first created man.

Now *a man* has fulfilled all righteousness. This was something that God was determined to see in his world.

41) <u>How is Jesus Christ related to the church?</u>

Jesus Christ is the Head of the Church.

> And he is the head of the body, the church; he is the beginning and the firstborn from among the dead, so that in everything he might have the supremacy. (Colossians 1:18)

Jesus was the first of the new kind of men to inhabit the eternal Kingdom of God. In himself, he laid the first steps for the foundation of the world to come: he became flesh and blood, then was crucified to destroy the first creation and its sin and death. Then he was resurrected to a new life with a body that can live in God's spiritual kingdom forever.

The rest of us must follow him in the same path that he took. To do this, we actually become *one* with him spiritually. This means that whatever Jesus enjoys now as a man in Heaven, will be ours as well. Our hope is certain because Jesus already sits in Heaven in our place – he draws his people into the reward that he bought for us there.

From his vantage point of the throne of authority and power in Heaven, he directs the growth of the Church. Church growth may seem haphazard to us, but Jesus is overseeing the entire process to make sure that every one of his children are included, cared for, and prepared for the Last Day.

Notes

Salvation

42) <u>How is a person saved?</u>

A person is saved by faith in Christ.

> That if you confess with your mouth, "Jesus is Lord," and believe in your heart that God raised him from the dead, you will be saved.
> (Romans 10:9)

There is no need for a sinner to do anything to please God in order to be saved – it wouldn't do any good anyway. His own works of righteousness – in other words, good works – aren't good enough to satisfy the complex and deep requirements of the Law. Besides, his past sin has already disqualified him from even trying to please God.

The only way that we can hope to come into God's presence and get forgiveness is if we take the offer of salvation in the finished work of Christ. He has fulfilled all the righteous requirements of the Law to God's satisfaction. Now all that we have to do is lay down our entire lives at his feet and surrender completely to him. As we do this, we find forgiveness for our sins, and the past is wiped away. And we discover that God is our Father who loves us and promises us eternal life with him.

All we need to do is call on Christ's name. He stands ready to respond to the sinner's cry for help and forgiveness. He is closer than we can imagine – all we have to do is call on him. Those who call on him can see that Jesus is our only hope of salvation from the wrath of God; and if we reach out to him, he *will* save us from sin and death.

43) <u>What is the first step of salvation?</u>

The first step of salvation is that our spirit is made alive to God.

> I tell you the truth, no one can see the
> kingdom of God unless he is born again.
> (John 3:3)

Every human being is born dead, spiritually. Their spirits are dead to God – they can't know him, they can't hear him speaking to them, they can't do anything to please him. The only things that they can "know" about God comes through tradition and hearsay.

This accounts for the fact that people don't know the truth about the real God, and they worship false gods instead. They don't know the danger that their souls are in spiritually, or their need to be saved from sin and death, or even how to be saved. They are blind to all this from birth.

But at conversion the Spirit of God gives new life to the dead spirit inside us. Now, as newborn children of God, we are aware of God and his spiritual world. We must grow in knowledge, of course, and with maturity we will learn how to live before God responsibly and in a way that pleases him. The point is that now we can see him, follow him, and obey him – all this is possible now to someone who formerly didn't know a thing about God. And spiritual growth is the best sign that we are now alive spiritually inside.

44) What is a Christian's relationship to Christ?

A Christian is made one with Christ.

> Since, then, you have been raised with Christ,
> set your hearts on things above, where Christ
> is seated at the right hand of God. Set your
> minds on things above, not on earthly things.
> For you died, and your life is now hidden with
> Christ in God. (Colossians 3:1-4)

Our salvation depends on a mystery. In a way that none of us can fully understand, but is real nonetheless, a person who is saved is made one with Christ. Spiritually, he finds that the life he lives is really Jesus living in him.

Whatever happens to Christ will happen to a child of God. The position that Jesus is in now, the privileges he enjoys, the life that he lives in Heaven, are now ours because we are in him spiritually. We don't understand *how* God can make us one with Christ, but our union with him is literally our salvation and very real.

Our lives are hidden in Christ, so that the world can no longer dominate us. A person who lives in this world is a citizen of this world, and therefore is under its dominion. But God has made his people citizens of Heaven, and they live in Christ. This means that they don't have to live under sin anymore. It also means that outward circumstances of this world have little or no impact on them, and certainly don't affect their spiritual standing in Heaven. You will often find persecuted saints in complete joy and peace, simply because they have learned to take advantage of their union with Christ who is above this world and its problems and trials.

45) Who saves us?

God saves us.

For it is by grace you have been saved, through faith — and this not from yourselves, it is the gift of God — not by works, so that no one can boast. (Ephesians 2:8-10)

Not only can we not save ourselves, we wouldn't even know where to start!

The Law is so deep and complex that we can't possibly know, or understand, how we have offended God with our sin. Jesus alone knows where and how we have gone wrong, and how to restore what we've ruined.

Our sin is so extensive and horrifying that we can't possibly make atonement for it, or satisfy God about it. Our crime is on the level of treachery – being a traitor to the King. Only the King himself can forgive a rebel and a traitor.

Our hearts are so deep that we can't know ourselves sufficiently to save ourselves. Though we might fully intend to do right, we will eventually go back to our old habits of sin because we can't help ourselves. Just when we think that we love God and are fully committed to him, something happens to reveal just how weak, rebellious and ignorant we are inside. Each day uncovers a new aspect of our hearts that shows how rebellious we really are. Only Jesus can see our hearts fully and apply a salvation that will cure us completely.

46) <u>What are we saved from?</u>

We are saved from our sins.

> She will give birth to a son, and you are to give him the name Jesus, because he will save his people from their sins. (Matthew 1:21)

Our fundamental problem is sin. All other problems in life come from this one root problem.

Because of our sin we suffer from disease, war, ignorance, sexual immorality, broken relationships, a ruined earth, murder, stealing, lying, and the complete range of ills that plague our society. Sin brings on death in many forms. It ruins nations as well as individuals. If we really understood this, we would work on the real problem instead of focusing on the effects of sin only.

Jesus came to address the problem of sin. At the top of his agenda is our sin; nothing else is as important to him as dealing with that. Though we might not want to keep turning to that issue, he is constantly bringing it up – first to save us from its dominion over us, and then for the rest of our lives to free us from its presence and deadly effects.

Living in the Spirit means to follow Jesus to the cross and get our sin crucified, wherever it lurks in our lives, and become holy in preparation for living in Heaven. Daily we are to present ourselves at his feet to be cleansed from our sin.

47) What did Jesus do for us legally?

Jesus made us fully justified before God.

> Therefore, since we have been justified through faith, we have peace with God through our Lord Jesus Christ, through whom we have gained access by faith into this grace in which we now stand. **(Romans 5:1-2)**

When Jesus saves someone, he not only makes that person's spirit alive to God, he also applies his own righteousness to his life. This has the effect of bringing someone into a new legal relationship with God.

Before a person is saved, he is a sinner and has nothing to hope for from God except condemnation and death because of his sin. Sin is rebellion against the King, and our situation is legally hopeless – unless we can present something to the Judge that will change his opinion of us.

What Jesus does is give us a perfect righteousness that will fully satisfy the Law. Clothed with the righteousness of Christ, God now looks at us as being acceptable to him, in a legal sense – he sees Jesus when he looks at us. Therefore he treats us legally as he does Jesus.

This is what "justification" means. Nothing we did or will do makes God feel better about us; it was what Jesus did that turned away the condemnation of the Law and brought legal acceptance from God. From now on, a child of God can expect full rights as a legal heir of the treasures of Heaven.

48) What is sanctification?

Sanctification is making a person ready for living in Heaven.

> And we, who with unveiled faces all reflect the Lord's glory, are being transformed into his likeness with ever-increasing glory, which comes from the Lord, who is the Spirit. (2 Corinthians 3:18)

Though a person is justified before God when he is first saved, there is still sin in his heart. Freedom from its dominion doesn't mean that we are free from its presence.

God expects his people to be holy, above all else. If he saves us legally from the Law's condemnation, he certainly intends to remove the reason for our getting ourselves into legal trouble in the first place —that is, our sin.

The job of the Spirit is to make us conform to the "righteous requirements of the Law." (Romans 8:4) As we follow the Spirit, he sanctifies us – which means that we surrender to the Lord, gradually lay aside our old way of life, and live for him alone.

God's goal is to make us fit for living with him in Heaven. There will be no sin in Heaven, therefore no sinners will be allowed in. Only those who have been made righteous in Christ, both legally and actually, will be allowed to live with God.

Notes

The Holy Spirit

49) What is the first thing that the Spirit does?

The Spirit reveals the truth of God to us.

> We have not received the spirit of the world but the Spirit who is from God, that we may understand what God has freely given us.
> (1 Corinthians 2:12)

This material world that we live in has been, to us, the only real world, according to our senses. The things that we value and the things that we own are in this world; the issues that we consider important are in this world; the people we respect are in this world; the forces that we fear are in this world. Most people live and die knowing nothing more than what is in this physical world, and they really don't care if there is another world – Heaven seems like an unrealistic story anyway, more like myths and fairy tales.

But the Spirit reveals, makes plain, uncovers, makes "seeable" the world that God lives in. It's like taking the veil away from a statue so that the public can see it for the first time. It's like opening a window into Heaven so that we can see inside God's house.

When we are born again, the Spirit opens our eyes so that we can see and know God. Now our knowledge of him isn't based on hearsay or tradition, but on direct, personal knowledge. And when we read the Bible, it becomes a means of communication for us: in it we hear God speaking to us, and using it we can talk to God directly through our prayers. The Spirit of God makes all of this possible.

50) What is the second thing that the Spirit does?

The Spirit empowers us to live in God's presence.

> **But you will receive power when the Holy Spirit comes on you; and you will be my witnesses in Jerusalem, and in all Judea and Samaria, and to the ends of the earth. (Acts 1:8)**

In order to live before God and not die, we have to change completely. In our physical state we can neither survive before God's glory, nor can we understand or appreciate what we would see there. Our physical senses weren't made to be aware of the things of God.

The Spirit gives life to our spirits – since our spirits *were* made to be aware of God and his world. That's why the Bible talks about having "eyes to see" and "ears to hear." The Spirit makes us alive spiritually so that our spiritual senses can start picking up on the things of God.

The Spirit helps us obey God – we find, as we follow the Spirit, that we can actually know and obey the commands that the Lord has given us. We find the spiritual strength to endure hardship; we find the spiritual skills to work in the Church for the building up of other Christians.

Through the Spirit we are enabled to "taste" the things of Heaven and begin enjoying our spiritual inheritance in Christ. While others suffer through the trials of this world, with no hope of things getting better, we eat and drink deeply at the table and wells of Heaven and rejoice in God's presence.

51) <u>Where does the Spirit lead us?</u>

The Spirit leads us to Heaven.

> **Instead, they were longing for a better country
> — a Heavenly one. Therefore God is not
> ashamed to be called their God, for he has
> prepared a city for them. (Hebrews 11:16)**

In order to fully understand what the Spirit is doing in our lives, we have to remember his two functions. The Spirit **reveals** the world of God to us – he shows us the spiritual Kingdom that God lives in, the one that we've been called to live in ourselves. And the Spirit **empowers** us to live in that Kingdom – God's world is of such a nature that the Spirit has to make us able to come into God's presence, able to take advantage of the treasures that God put in Christ for us. In other words, the primary focus of the Spirit in our lives is to make us fit to live in the Kingdom of God.

We have begun a journey: from the moment that we woke up spiritually and saw our Savior, the rest of our lives will be a steady progress from earth to Heaven. And the Spirit is doing two things for us: *first*, he will keep us in the right path – the way that Jesus himself walked. And *second*, he is slowly making us fit to arrive there in perfect condition and pleasing to our Master.

Our lives *will* change. We will be less involved with this world, and will become more interested in the next one. We are in the process of leaving this world – and that should become more apparent to others as time goes on.

52) How must we worship God?

We must worship God in Spirit.

> God is Spirit, and his worshipers must
> worship in Spirit and in truth. (John 4:24)

God requires us to worship him in Spirit and in truth. The truth, of course, is the Bible. In order to approach God, we have to know him and what we can expect from him. That's what the Bible does for us.

But to worship God in Spirit is more difficult to understand, because we can't simply turn the Spirit on and off at will. If we keep in mind, however, the two functions of the Spirit – that he reveals and empowers – the answer is clearer to see.

Our duty is to come to God in Heaven, to his throne, into his actual presence. We need things from the spiritual treasury in Christ, and we have to get our orders from the King. Worship isn't a formal ceremony; it's what Hebrews 12 describes as actually coming into the presence of God – by means of the Bible – so that we can have real communication with the living God. The Spirit leads us to the real God of the Bible; and there God gives us his spiritual treasures to equip us for our lives and work.

True worship means coming to God and giving him the glory he deserves, and being filled with spiritual food and drink from Heaven's storehouses.

53) Where is the Spirit now?

The Spirit lives in a believer's heart.

> **And this is how we know that he lives in us:**
> **We know it by the Spirit he gave us.**
> **(1 John 3:24)**

Jesus returned to Heaven to sit at God's right hand, on God's throne. But he promised that he would never be far away from his people. The way he keeps that promise is by sending his Spirit to live in their hearts.

Not only does the Spirit wake up our spirits so that we can become aware of God, but the Spirit dwells in us to keep that connection with God alive. At no point is a believer so far away from the Lord that his prayers won't be heard. The resources of Heaven are always near for those who ask for them.

And since this is the Spirit of Christ in us, we find that Jesus lives his life through us. When we are too weak or ignorant to obey God, Jesus fills us with his own life, strength and wisdom and makes us able to do things that we could never do on our own.

Since the Spirit lives *in* us, he will guide us in the way we have to go. All we have to do is follow the Spirit, keep in step with the Spirit, walk in the Spirit wherever he leads us. He will make it plain to us where he wants us to go. But if we rebel against his gentle but sure leading, this will grieve the Spirit and God will have to deal with our sin before we can continue on the way.

Notes

The Kingdom of God

54) What is the message of the Gospel?

The Gospel is the good news of the Kingdom of God.

> "The time has come," he said. "The kingdom of God is near. Repent and believe the good news!" (Mark 1:15)

When Jesus began to preach, he announced the coming of the Kingdom of God.

The prophet's role was to announce to his audience that there was a King coming, and he is bringing his army with him. The king will judge all the wicked, destroy the immoral kingdoms of the earth, and set up his own righteous kingdom in their place.

Jesus himself was a Prophet like Moses (see Deuteronomy 18:15), and his role was to announce the coming of a new kind of Kingdom – a spiritual Kingdom that would finally put an end to all earthly kingdoms. The "good news" is that he is giving us a chance to change sides before the King gets here with his army to destroy the earth. We have a chance *now* to repent and plead for his mercy. If we do that, he is faithful and just and will forgive us our sins against him. He will also make us one of his own children, and arm us to fight in the coming battle on his side.

But we must act now while we have a chance to switch sides. Those who repent will find the King to be "merciful and gracious ... forgiving wickedness, rebellion and sin." And he will make us part of his new spiritual Kingdom, which is real life compared to the sin, darkness and death of this world.

55) What must we do to enter the Kingdom of God?

To enter the Kingdom of God, we must repent and believe in the King, Jesus Christ.

> **Believe in the Lord Jesus, and you will be saved – you and your household. (Acts 16:31)**

The reason that the King is coming with his army is to destroy this world. Man has filled the world with sin, ignorance, death, misery, suffering, wars, and depravity. This isn't the world that the Creator made in the beginning! And since the best solution is to simply wipe the slate clean and start over, the King is bringing the hosts of the army of Heaven to destroy the world's kingdoms.

The King intends to destroy all who are on the wrong side of the battlefield. Satan is the "ruler of the kingdom of the air," and everyone who is Satan's child or slave will be destroyed along with him.

But there's a chance to "escape the wrath to come." If a person repents – which means he/she has to turn their back on sin, on this world, and on the lies of the enemy and turn their eyes and heart on Jesus the Savior – then the King will receive them as one of his own. They have to admit that their life so far has been service to the wrong king; they have to admit that their hearts are incurably wicked and they need the miraculous hand of God to fix their hearts.

If someone does that, they're ready to switch sides – and Jesus will re-make their heart to be able to love and serve God. He makes them citizens of Heaven and children of God.

56) What is the King doing now?

The King is putting all things in this world under his feet.

> **Then the end will come, when he hands over the kingdom to God the Father after he has destroyed all dominion, authority and power. For he must reign until he has put all his enemies under his feet. The last enemy to be destroyed is death. (1 Corinthians 15:24-27)**

The Kingdom of God isn't going to take over the world overnight. It will come gradually: step by step, the Lord will claim more repentant souls, and add to his ranks more soldiers of the Cross to form his Church. Gradually the ranks of the People of God will swell to a mighty host.

Each new convert is a spiritual stone that the Lord uses to build his eternal Temple, where he intends to live forever. As they become part of the Church, they are given the Spirit of God for two reasons: first, to enable them to receive spiritual nourishment from Heaven; and second, to make them skilled for the work of building the Kingdom as co-laborers with Christ.

The Kingdom isn't advancing along geographical or political lines – it advances among all people. Many hear the offer of the King in the Gospel, a few like the idea, even fewer are actually changed in heart to be a spiritual part of the new Kingdom.

57) <u>What does the King give us in his kingdom?</u>

The King gives us righteousness, peace, and joy in the Holy Spirit.

> **For the kingdom of God is not a matter of eating and drinking, but of righteousness, peace and joy in the Holy Spirit. (Romans 14:17)**

The Kingdom that Jesus intends to build is a spiritual Kingdom. It's not like the physical kingdoms of the world.

What man has done to God's original creation is ruin a perfect world. Instead of using and enjoying what God created, man twisted it to his own ends – and ruined it in the process. The "world" of man's making only produces hurt, suffering, more sin, and death. And Satan tempts each generation into ruining the world even worse than in previous generations.

But Jesus is building a Kingdom that can't be touched by sin or death. In his Kingdom there's going to be justice, and everyone will be perfect and righteous according to the standards of God's holy Law. Christ will rule as the perfect King – governing his people with justice, doing everything he can to promote their welfare and happiness, loving them deeply as his own people whom he would defend with his life. In all his Kingdom there will be no more crying or suffering or pain or death; the old ruined world will pass away forever, and he will rule among his people in a new spiritual world in which everyone will know, enjoy, and serve God wholeheartedly.

58) What is our duty to the King?

Our duty is to obey the King and serve him in all things with all of our lives.

> **Your kingdom come, your will be done on earth as it is in Heaven. (Matthew 6:10)**

A Christian understands that his purpose in life is to serve and obey his God. Everything else is secondary in importance.

Man was first designed to serve God. He was supposed to rule over God's creation as the image of God – which means that he would rule as God rules, with God's wisdom and aiming at God's goals. In order to do this, Adam would have to maintain constant contact with God in order to know the will of God, in order to carry out that will on earth as his representative. He wasn't supposed to have his own will!

Adam failed, but now in Christ we have a second chance. Again, Jesus is the King – and our job is to carry out his will on earth as he builds his Kingdom among us. Jesus has all wisdom, authority and power; our job is to open the door to that Heavenly wisdom and power so that it can be felt in our world. Our calling is to provide opportunities for the work of God on earth.

We must put our own opinions and will aside, we must pray for his will, we must step aside, wait on him, and let him do his own work in our lives. We must provide opportunities for the work of God to continue among us. The more that God himself does through us, the more glory he gets from it, and the better we serve him.

Notes

Faith

59) What is faith?

Faith is walking in the light of God's world.

> Now faith is being sure of what we hope for and certain of what we do not see. (Hebrews 11:1)

In our natural state, we are born into spiritual darkness. We don't know the true God, nor can we get in touch with him. The only things we "know" about God are what people have told us.

But when we are "born again," the Spirit opens our eyes so that we can see the Lord Jesus. Suddenly a story becomes a real person. There is a real confrontation in which we see his glory, feel thoroughly ashamed because of our sin, confess and repent of our sin against him – and then he reaches out and makes us whole.

That initial encounter with the Lord isn't the end of it, though. From that point on we live in the light that Heaven sends down around us. Through the Bible and the Spirit, we can now see our God, we know how to obey and honor him, and we know where we are headed in life – to be with him in Heaven.

We can also see our way around this dark world. We can see the spiritual dangers and pitfalls that other people stumble into. We know our real enemy now, because we can see his influence and see the damage he does to men's souls.

And faith isn't something that we can grasp if we want it – no more than a blind man can see. God has to open the eyes of the soul so that we can see the light of Heaven.

60) How must a believer live in this world?

A believer lives by faith, not by sight.

> We live by faith, not by sight.
> (2 Corinthians 5:7)

God made the world with two sides – physical and spiritual. Our physical senses were designed to know the physical world, but our spiritual senses – the senses of the soul – were designed to know God's spiritual world.

In our sinful state, we are dead to God's spiritual world. That's why so many people plunge right into sin and wickedness and never know why things fall apart in their lives. It's like a blind man stepping out into a busy highway.

But when we are given the gift of faith, we can see many things that we need to know in order to live for God. We can see his glory and how to glorify him ourselves; we can see our own souls, and why we need to change in order to please a holy God. We can see Jesus and what we need in him to be saved. We can feel the Holy Spirit leading us in a sure and direct route to Heaven. We can see the dangers and pitfalls of this world that so many people can't see and fall into. We can see the works and ways of the devil – we know how to resist him.

Therefore, with this new spiritual sight, we must walk in the light of this spiritual world. The only way we can see it is, of course, through the Bible and the leading of the Spirit. That's why we have to stay in constant touch with that world through these means.

61) With whom is a Christian at war?

A Christian is at war with the forces of darkness.

> For our struggle is not against flesh and blood, but against the rulers, against the authorities, against the powers of this dark world and against the spiritual forces of evil in the heavenly realms. (Ephesians 6:10-13)

We tend to think that our enemies are our neighbors – people who do things to us that we don't like. That's the cause of most of the wars and feuds of the world; we're often fighting the wrong enemy.

The enemy is the devil. From the beginning he has tried to destroy God's creation, especially man. And his principal weapon is lying and deceit. By tempting man into sin with the lie "you can do this and nothing will happen to you," he successfully leads people into sin against God and the required punishment of death.

Someone who has true faith is going to see the real enemy and the tactics he uses. He's going to see that other people are being used by the enemy for his terrible work. Not that sinners who are duped by the devil are innocent; he only appeals to their sinful nature that's already there. But people are still redeemable, if only they will respond to the Gospel and switch masters.

Faith enables us to see the tactics that the enemy uses and find appropriate resources from Heaven to counteract them. Someone who is walking in faith is done with sin, and he will no longer fall prey to the enemy of his soul. He has the victory over sin, death, the world, and the devil.

62) Where is the Christian's citizenship?

A Christian's citizenship is in Heaven.

> And they admitted that they were aliens and strangers on earth. People who say such things show that they are looking for a country of their own. (Hebrews 11:13-14)

At the beginning, man was created to serve God on earth. But because of sin and death, and the fall of the entire world into suffering and destruction, the plan has changed. From now on, God is preparing a place in Heaven for his people to live.

Two things show us this: **first**, Jesus, after his resurrection, returned to Heaven for the purpose of preparing a home for us there. A man went into Heaven! As a man, he's getting a place ready that we can live in. And the place he has in mind will be at the right hand of the throne of God, far above all other creatures who live there.

Second, the Spirit is busy changing us for that great day to come when we will change worlds. Flesh and blood can't go into Heaven as they are and survive. We have to be changed – our souls have to wake up and become aware of God, for example. What good would it do us to go to Heaven and not be able to see or know God? Our hearts have to be cleansed of their sin. We have to learn the manners and ways of Heaven – to become holy, and skilled at serving God.

So while we live and work in this world, our hearts are in another world already. It's only a matter of time till we leave this temporary home for our eternal one.

63) What must our faith produce?

Faith must produce deeds.

> As the body without the spirit is dead, so
> faith without deeds is dead. (James 2:26)

Our Christian faith means nothing if it's just a lot of spiritual notions in our heads. If we simply believe something to be true, yet we don't act on it as if it's true, then what good is our belief? If we act as if this world is all that is important, yet we say that we are looking forward to Heaven, who will be convinced with our so-called faith?

True faith will motivate us to live as if God's world is real, and our hearts need saving, and the devil is really at work to destroy us. True faith will lead us to save up riches in Heaven and turn our backs on this world's pleasures and wealth. True faith will make it plain what our duty is when we are faced with decisions to make – either work for our own pleasures and interests, or work for God's Kingdom.

And true faith will reach out to others in a way that proves that we see the real spiritual situation. If someone is a brother or sister in Christ, and they are in need, someone with faith isn't going to let them go without the basic necessities of life. If someone is persecuting us for our faith, we aren't going to lash back at them in anger – we're going to see the real enemy behind this poor deluded sinner and try to win him over to our side.

Our works don't *make* us Christians; they only prove that we *are* Christians. God has to change our hearts first if we want to be saved. But a changed heart is going to live in this world in a different way than someone whose heart isn't changed.

Notes

The Church

64) What is the Church?

The Church is the body of Christ.

> Now you are the body of Christ, and each one
> of you is a part of it. (1 Corinthians 12:27)

When someone becomes a Christian, they don't exist all on their own – as if they are a single spiritual entity adrift in a big universe. They become united with Christ himself, spiritually, and they take their place alongside others with the same faith in the Lord. Jesus literally lives his life in all of us, in our hearts. Because we are one with him, everything that he experiences and receives from the Father is also true of us.

The key is that all believers are part of Christ – which makes us all one body. As in a physical body, not every believer serves the same function. Each person plays his or her own role in the Church. But we are all experiencing the life of Christ as he lives before the Father in Heaven. As the Lord builds his eternal house, he adds new stones to build up the walls – and each Christian is a "living stone" (1 Peter 2:15) who takes his place in the great work that God is building.

Christians often think that they can't get along with each other. Denominations, the modern curse of the Church, divide brothers and sisters over issues that shouldn't be the source of war among us. The Lord gave us his Spirit to make us *one* in faith and life, and we should be sharing what makes us common instead of focusing on minor differences. As one body we have a great work to do in this world: to help build the Kingdom of God.

65) What are spiritual gifts?

Spiritual gifts are special skills given by Christ to build up the Church.

> It was he who gave some to be apostles, some to be prophets, some to be evangelists, and some to be pastors and teachers, to prepare God's people for works of service.
> (Ephesians 4:11-13)

The Church has several jobs to do: *first*, it's a spiritual nursery to raise new Christians. People have to be trained in the doctrines of the faith, and shown how to lead a life pleasing to the Father. *Second*, the Church is an armed force called to do battle against the enemy. *Third*, the Church is God's witness on earth to show the entire world who the real God is and what man's duty to him is.

In order to do these jobs, Christians need extraordinary wisdom, strength and skill. This work will require the mind and power of God that can overcome the forces of darkness. That's where the Spirit of God comes in: he provides the wisdom and power to do what we are called to do. Without him we are powerless to change our world; with him, we can do even the things that Jesus did. (John 14:12)

The Spirit enables each person to do a specific job in the Church. In any one body of Christians, the Lord will provide the necessary gifts for that church. Leaders are supposed to be on the lookout for those gifts and get them operating for the benefit of the whole group. A well-balanced, healthy church will be full of busy laborers all doing their work – which is making Christ present and known among men.

66) What should the "normal" church look like?

The "normal" church should look like the pattern in Acts 2.

> **They devoted themselves to the apostles' teaching and to the fellowship, to the breaking of bread and to prayer. (Acts 2:42-47)**

Though most people don't think that there is such a thing as a "normal" church – they don't think it's possible – the example in Acts proves that idea wrong. The apostles' church was made up of sinners (as our churches are), who are filled with the Spirit (as we ought to be), taking their calling from God seriously (which we don't often do, unfortunately).

These four functions (as well as the activities that follow in that passage) make a healthy church. Will there be problems in every church in this world? Certainly! But isn't God faithful in providing the treasures of Heaven to solve those problems? Didn't Jesus promise to send his Spirit among us so that we can obey him and help build his Kingdom? So if our churches aren't healthy, if they aren't accomplishing the work that the Master has given us, it isn't fair to blame the Lord – our own sins are preventing us from experiencing his blessing in church.

Too often our culture dictates to us what is "possible" and what isn't "reasonable" when it comes to church life. But there's nothing keeping us from doing it God's way – which is the way described here in Acts. A church like this will have the power to change its culture and finally start solving the cultural ills that surround us.

67) What is the Church Universal?

The Church Universal consists of all believers around the world, through all time.

> Here there is no Greek or Jew, circumcised or uncircumcised, barbarian, Scythian, slave or free, but Christ is all, and is in all.
> (Colossians 3:11)

The old word for "universal" used to be "catholic." Unfortunately, because the Roman Catholic church was the only church around for a thousand years, some misunderstand the word "catholic" in the Apostles' Creed to mean the Roman church. "Catholic" in the Apostles' day simply meant the "universal" church.

And "universal" doesn't mean what the Roman church means by it (in other words, all the RC's who belong to their denomination). Christ's church is his body, which is the entire group of spiritual children of God all around the world, and all through history. The Church of Christ includes saved souls who aren't necessarily in one denomination or another, or who don't necessarily hold to a certain creed. All they need is that simple faith in Christ that he is their Savior from sin and death, and the heart made new by the Spirit.

The making of a Christian is a simple matter. Someone hears the truth about Christ, sees his or her need of him, repents and is forgiven. Jesus opens their eyes and gives life to their spirits. Now they are members of the body of Christ, no matter what church they may belong to.

68) <u>What happens when Christians meet together?</u>

When Christians meet together, Christ dwells among them.

> For where two or three come together in my name, there am I with them. (Matthew 18:20)

A meeting of Christians isn't like a club of members getting together because they share the same interests. Something mystical happens among Christians: according to Christ's promise, he appears among them, through his Spirit.

The reason for this is that the goals of a church meeting are beyond the normal human abilities to achieve. *First*, they come together to worship God. But only through the Spirit lifting them up into Heaven, into God's presence, can they achieve that goal. *Second*, they need the spiritual food and other treasures that Jesus has for them in Heaven. But only by the Spirit filling them in the meeting, and through the ministry that each member has for the whole group, will they be able to get their spiritual needs met.

This doesn't always happen, unfortunately, when people meet together in a church. Often they have lost touch with the Lord in their personal walk with Jesus, or the church has strayed away from its spiritual calling, so that Jesus refuses to acknowledge that group as his church, no matter what they call themselves. (See Revelation 2:5 for his threat to leave a dead church.) His promise is for those who keep his commands, who worship in the Spirit, and who have made themselves holy by his blood.

Notes

Judgment Day

69) When is the Last Day?

Nobody knows when the Last Day will be.

> No one knows about that day or hour, not even the angels in Heaven, nor the Son, but only the Father. Be on guard! Be alert! You do not know when that time will come.
> (Mark 13:32-33)

So many people have made the mistake of trying to predict when the Lord will come back and the world as we know it will end. Generation after generation have tried to pin down the exact date of the Lord's return. And each prediction has come to nothing.

When even Jesus himself didn't know when the Last Day would be, it's a bad idea to try to figure it out without him. The lesson here is that we are worried about the *wrong thing*: instead of spending so much time on *when* Jesus will return, we ought to be getting ourselves *ready* for his return.

Very few of us are going to be alive when Jesus returns. Much of the fascination over when he's coming is only because people would rather focus on the sensational mysteries of the Bible instead of the state of their hearts. Many who are worried about the time of Christ's return won't be ready spiritually to meet him when he does return.

The warning of Scripture is always this: *get yourself ready for his return.* We only have a few short years to do that. If we prepare our hearts to live with God in Heaven, it won't matter if Jesus waits a million years to come back – he will come back for us according to his promise.

70) How will Jesus Christ come back the second time?

Jesus Christ will come back visibly, in power and glory.

> For the Lord himself will come down from heaven, with a loud command, with the voice of the archangel and with the trumpet call of God ... (1 Thessalonians 4:16)

Jesus intends to come back visibly, as a person, in the same way he came the first time. But this second coming will be *in glory* this time. People aren't going to mistake who he is. This time they will see the King, the Creator, the Savior, the Redeemer, the Son of God. They will fear him as they ought. The children of God will recognize their Savior and rejoice at his coming; the wicked will recognize their Judge and dread his coming.

His first coming confused a lot of people. They didn't realize that he was the King and Savior and Creator – all they saw was Mary's son, born in a strange way (for all they knew he was illegitimate!). Jesus was known as the carpenter's son, one of the boys from Nazareth – the Pharisees didn't even know he was born in Bethlehem!

But his second coming won't be confusing at all. He is going to finish the job he started – putting all his enemies under his feet, burning up the first heavens and earth (2 Peter 3), and bringing all souls before the Judgment Seat. He is coming in power and glory, with the hosts of Heaven at his back. And his coming will be sudden, unannounced, and un-looked for – to the dismay of those who aren't ready.

71) What will happen to Christians when Jesus comes back?

The dead will be raised from their graves and made alive, and the living will be changed, and we shall all rise to meet Jesus in the air.

> ... and the dead in Christ will rise first. After that, we who are still alive and are left will be caught up together with them in the clouds to meet the Lord in the air. And so we will be with the Lord forever. (1 Thessalonians 4:16-17)

The reason he's coming back is to wind up this world's affairs and start the next phase of God's plan – the eternal home of the righteous. All Christians will rise into Heaven to live with God forever. The life that Jesus bought with his own blood will now be theirs: eternal, holy, full of joy and peace, and in the presence of God himself. All the riches and treasures of Heaven will belong to them.

Christians who are already dead will come out alive from their graves; Christians who are still alive when he returns will be lifted up in the air, changed into spiritual beings, and will take their place behind him among the armies of Heaven. From that point on the people of God will be part of a new world, a new life with Christ in the presence of God, never to be separated from him again.

The point is that we are not going to be left in the grave. Jesus is going to reverse the curse of death and bring about a general resurrection from the dead, the greatest miracle of the end times. After this there will be no more death.

72) <u>Who is going to be judged?</u>

Every human being will be judged.

> For we must all appear before the judgment
> seat of Christ, that each one may receive
> what is due him for the things done while in
> the body, whether good or bad.
> (2 Corinthians 5:10)

A common mistake that many people make is that they think they won't be judged on Judgment Day – they have already believed in Christ, and now they feel that God will just take them directly to the joys of Heaven when they die. They don't understand the purpose of Judgment Day. On that day, God intends to uncover the truth about his works, his ways, our hearts, and the events of history. Judgment isn't necessarily a negative thing – on the contrary, it will be a day of glory for God's people. The only people who have reason to fear Judgment Day are the wicked.

When Christ saves a soul, he does such an amazing work that the story deserves telling. Usually, however, nobody really knows all the details of what happened between sinner and Savior – not even the person who was saved. The whole story ought to be told in detail if God is going to get credit for what he did, and all the worship that he deserves.

So not only are the wicked going to be brought before the Judge of all the earth to be examined and rejected (and everyone will agree that his judgment on them will be just) but so will God's people be brought to have their hearts revealed. Then the story of their salvation will be told fully, and everyone will agree that their reward to enter Heaven will be entirely appropriate.

73) What will God finally get on Judgment Day?

God will finally get the glory he deserves on Judgment Day.

> That at the name of Jesus every knee should bow, in heaven and on earth and under the earth, and every tongue confess that Jesus Christ is Lord, to the glory of God the Father. (Philippians 2:10-11)

God deserves much more glory than he gets. He is responsible for an enormous amount of what goes on in this world – he made it, he takes care of it daily, and he is preparing it for the next stage of the divine plan.

The problem is that he gets little or no glory for what he does. This amounts to slapping him in the face – this God who gave us all life and breath! Such an injustice isn't going to last forever, however. On Judgment Day – which God is looking forward to – it will all be revealed what God did for us. We will be forced to see everything in history in great detail, and we will know then what we have ignored all along. God will finally get all the credit that is due him.

This is important because, unless God makes it plain what he did, and why he did it, we probably will accuse him of being unjust in making us go through the problems we had, or at least so weak and impotent that he couldn't take care of us properly! When he reveals the truth about his works and ways, we will all know then that he was right and good, and we just didn't understand.

Notes

Heaven and Hell

74) <u>What is Heaven?</u>

Heaven is the place of God's throne, and the eternal home of his people.

> Now the dwelling of God is with men, and he will live with them. They will be his people, and God himself will be with them and be their God. (Revelation 21:3)

Heaven is a spiritual place. It's the house of God, so it's going to have the same characteristics that God has: eternal, holy, a place of peace, righteousness, and so on. God insists that the environment of his own home have the same qualities as himself.

This means that anyone who intends to live with God must also have the same qualities. In order for sinners to enter Heaven, they must first be made holy and righteous just as God is. This can only be done by the blood of the Lamb, and the work of the Holy Spirit on their spirits. But once they've been made ready, they will "shine like stars" and take their place beside God as his children.

Christians have a special hope in Heaven: there they will live in the presence of God, and get everything they need directly from God's hand. In this world we are used to getting what we need through created things; but in Heaven everything we need will come directly from God himself. There will be no more need of sun or moon, food or water, and the other things that we needed here – the Lord God himself will be our food, light and life.

75) What is waiting for us in Heaven?

There is a room in Heaven for each of God's children that Jesus has been preparing for us.

> I am going there to prepare a place for you. And if I go and prepare a place for you, I will come back and take you to be with me that you also may be where I am. (John 14:2-3)

Jesus left this world for two reasons: *first*, to assume the throne of Heaven and, from there, direct the affairs of nations and the Church through his Spirit. *Second*, he is getting our home ready for the day of our own arrival in Heaven.

What will that home be like if it takes the Almighty Creator of the world (who made the first world, remember, in six days!) over 2000 years to get it ready for us? The great wisdom of Christ, and the unlimited power of Christ, and his love for us which knows no limits, is building an eternal Temple that will be beyond our imagination.

God intends to live with his people. He showed us how much he wanted to live with us in the Old Testament pictures of the Temple in Jerusalem. Saints like David knew the tremendous privilege it was to live so near God – there would be no end of the joy, peace and fellowship that one can have with the Almighty when we are so close to him. In Heaven we will be one with Christ, and nothing will separate us from his presence. There we will finally know the ecstasy of the human soul, what we were made for in the beginning – to know God as he is.

76) What will Christians be in Heaven?

Christians will be the heirs of God in Heaven.

> He who overcomes will inherit all this, and I
> will be his God and he will be my son.
> (Revelation 21:7)

The staggering truth of the Christian's hope in Heaven is beyond our comprehension. Even the angels wonder at the free grace of God to such sinners as we.

God gave us a gift in Christ: through faith we can become one with Jesus, the only Son of God. Now whatever Jesus gets while in Heaven, we also get. If he stands beside God's throne, then so will we. If he is the heir of all the treasures of God in Heaven, then so are we his heirs. Of course we are also going to be made righteous and holy as Jesus is, because nobody can be made one with Christ and inherit the treasures of Heaven unless they are perfect.

Paul says that we have been adopted by God – we who were sinners and had no right to the hope of Heaven, have been brought into God's family and given all the legal rights as sons.

What will we do as God's children? *First*, we will be closer to him, and enjoy him more, than any other creature in Heaven. *Second*, we ourselves will sit on Christ's throne with him and rule over God's Kingdom – just as Adam was made to be a ruler in the beginning.

77) How can a person get to Heaven?

To enter Heaven, you must believe in the Lord Jesus Christ as Savior and King.

> That if you confess with your mouth, "Jesus is Lord," and believe in your heart that God raised him from the dead, you will be saved.
> (Romans 10:9)

People are very confused about how to get into Heaven, even though the Bible makes it very plain and clear. We can't go to Heaven because of our own works of goodness; our sins have already put us in a dangerous legal position so that no amount of good works can overcome that.

Our only hope is if we can go there on the back, so to speak, of someone else who *does* have the right to enter. You must come to Jesus, bow down before him in submission, repent of the sinfulness and wickedness of your heart, give yourself wholly to him, and ask him to forgive you and cleanse you of your sin. And the reason you come to him is because you know he has the authority and power to save you.

This simple transaction between you and the living Christ is all that is needed. From the point when he reaches out and touches your soul with his Spirit and saves you (you'll know when he does!), you belong to him. As he leads the way to Heaven, you follow him. Do what he does; lean on him to lead you and rescue you and change you; go where he goes. He literally becomes your shepherd who guides you to eternal life. And when you come to the Judgment seat, you will find that he already took care of your past sins – you will be allowed in solely because you belong to the Master.

78) <u>What is Hell?</u>

Hell is the eternal punishment of the wicked.

> **He will punish those who do not know God and do not obey the gospel of our Lord Jesus. They will be punished with everlasting destruction and shut out from the presence of the Lord and from the majesty of his power. (2 Thessalonians 1:8-9)**

God made very plain to man, from the beginning of the world, what his duties and responsibilities are. The Law is clear and easy to understand. But man willfully made himself blind and hardened to the Law's demands. So when man deliberately turns his back on his Creator, there is only one thing to do: punish the lawbreaker. And that's what Hell is – a punishment of someone who knew what he had to do and yet refused to do it. It's an appropriate sentence for a willful crime.

Hell is terrible. And the purpose of the message of Hell in the Bible is to terrify sinners into repentance. The picture of Hell that we are given in the Bible is found in Mark 9:48 – "the worm that does not die, and the fire that is not quenched." The worm is symbolic of the breakdown and decay of the physical body after it's put in the grave. It's also symbolic of the eternal destruction of the soul. Fire is a symbol of the torment of the soul in eternity.

The soul that is in eternal torment is fully conscious of itself, its sufferings, and even knows about Heaven! Much of the agony comes from the constant awareness of God's wrath against them. In short, you don't want to go there!

79) <u>What was Hell made for?</u>

Hell was first made as a punishment for the devil and his angels.

> **Depart from me, you who are cursed, into the eternal fire prepared for the devil and his angels. (Matthew 25:41)**

Hell was first made for the devil and his angels. As the first rebels against the Creator, they have the dubious honor of being destined for eternal agony. They have no chance at all of escaping their doom; none of them will ever have a chance to repent of their sin.

Man wasn't supposed to go to Hell – he was made to honor God, not to rebel against him. But when Adam plunged the entire human race into sin, he wrote a sentence of doom over most of his descendents. They, like their father, turn their backs on their Creator just as Satan did.

There are several sins mentioned in the Bible that will condemn a person to Hell: ***first***, for rebelling against God the Creator and worshiping false gods; ***second***, for rejecting Jesus Christ as the Savior from our sin; ***third***, for not showing mercy to the children of God (as this story in Matthew 25 shows!); ***fourth***, for those who caused Christ's children to sin; ***fifth***, for those who don't use the skills and talents to do the job that God gave them to do.

Though most people don't believe in Hell, that won't help them escape the penalty on Judgment Day. God's perfect justice will only be satisfied when the wicked are justly punished for their crimes against a holy God.

80) How long does Hell last?

Hell lasts forever.

> They will be punished with everlasting destruction and shut out from the presence of the Lord and from the majesty of his power. (2 Thessalonians 1:9)

Many people think that Hell, if there is such a place, won't last long. Or at least it will be like the medieval idea of Purgatory – a punishment that may last for thousands of years, but it will come to an end eventually.

But things don't work like that in God's court. The sentence of Hell that he will hand out to the wicked will be an eternal sentence. When a million years of their suffering has gone by, they have only begun to feel the wrath of the King. There will be no reprieve, no hope of change, no relenting of the severity of the sentence. Their destruction will be forever.

This is perhaps the hardest part about Hell for people to accept. They don't like the idea of the wrath of God, but they could accept even that if there were some hope of that terrible anger coming to an end someday. But the Bible teaches the eternal nature of Hell plainly.

The reason God wills this is because of the nature of the crime against him. When a person turns his back on his Creator, he tears apart God's purposes, denying God's infinite wisdom, rebelling against God's perfect Law, and substituting wickedness and death in the place of God's life and righteousness. Thanks to man and his sin, there's an enormous amount of suffering and death and destruction in God's world. Someone has to pay for this mess.

Notes

The Apostles' Creed

The Apostles' Creed has been a standard of doctrine and belief for the Christian Church since near her beginning.

The Creed isn't actually the production of the Apostles. It was a summary of the teaching of the Apostles that the Early Church Fathers put together to help Christians learn the basics of the faith.

The Apostles' Creed contains all the necessary elements for true Christianity. Someone who believes these things can truly call himself a believer in Christ as the Bible describes; someone who has problems with these points can't honestly claim to be a Christian. It is the one statement of faith that all Christian churches, no matter what their denomination, can share.

I believe in God the Father Almighty, maker of Heaven and earth, and in Jesus Christ his only-begotten Son, our Lord:

Who was conceived by the Holy Spirit, born of the virgin Mary, suffered under Pontius Pilate, was crucified, dead, and buried. The third day he rose again from the dead; he ascended into Heaven, and sits at the right hand of God the Father Almighty. From thence he shall come to judge the living and the dead.

I believe in the Holy Spirit, the holy catholic[1] Church, the communion of saints, the forgiveness of sins, the resurrection of the body, and the life everlasting. Amen.

---

[1] "Catholic" meaning "universal," not the Roman Church.

The Lord's Prayer

Commonly known as the Lord's Prayer, Jesus taught his disciples to pray with these words that are recorded in Matthew 6:9-13.

Our Father in Heaven, hallowed be your Name,

Your Kingdom come, your will be done on earth as it is in Heaven.

Give us today our daily bread.

Forgive us our debts, as we also have forgiven our debtors.

And lead us not into temptation, but deliver us from the evil one.

For yours is the Kingdom, the power, and the glory forever. Amen.

www.ingramcontent.com/pod-product-compliance
Lightning Source LLC
La Vergne TN
LVHW011241080426
835509LV00005B/582

* 9 7 8 0 6 1 5 1 3 9 3 2 6 *